BOUNDARIES
in Dating

Resources by Henry Cloud and John Townsend

Boundaries
Boundaries Workbook
Boundaries audio
Boundaries video curriculum
Boundaries in Dating
Boundaries in Dating Workbook
Boundaries in Dating audio
Boundaries in Dating video curriculum
Boundaries in Marriage
Boundaries in Marriage Workbook
Boundaries in Marriage audio
Boundaries with Kids
Boundaries with Kids Workbook
Boundaries with Kids audio
Changes That Heal (Cloud)
Changes That Heal Workbook (Cloud)
Changes That Heal audio (Cloud)
Hiding from Love (Townsend)
The Mom Factor
The Mom Factor Workbook
The Mom Factor audio
Raising Great Kids
Raising Great Kids for Parents of Preschoolers curriculum
Raising Great Kids Workbook for Parents of Preschoolers
Raising Great Kids Workbook for Parents of School-Age Children
Raising Great Kids Workbook for Parents of Teenagers
Raising Great Kids audio
Safe People
Safe People Workbook
Safe People audio
Twelve "Christian" Beliefs That Can Drive You Crazy

Making Dating Work

BOUNDARIES
in Dating

PARTICIPANT'S GUIDE

Dr. Henry Cloud & Dr. John Townsend
with Lisa Guest

ZondervanPublishingHouse
Grand Rapids, Michigan

A Division of HarperCollinsPublishers

Boundaries in Dating Participant's Guide
Copyright © 2001 by Henry Cloud and John Townsend

Requests for information should be addressed to:

 ZondervanPublishingHouse
Grand Rapids, Michigan 49530

ISBN 0-310-23875-7

All Scripture quotations unless otherwise noted are taken from the *Holy Bible: New International Version*®. NIV®. Copyright © 1973, 1978, 1984 by International Bible Society. Used by permission of Zondervan Publishing House. All rights reserved.

All rights reserved. No part of this publication may be reproduced, stored in a retrieval system, or transmitted in any form or by any means—electronic, mechanical, photocopy, recording, or any other—except for brief quotations in printed reviews, without the prior permission of the publisher.

Published in association with Yates & Greer, LLP, Literary Agent, Orange, CA.

Interior design by Rob Monacelli

Printed in the United States of America

00 01 02 03 04 05 /❖ DC/ 10 9 8 7 6 5 4 3 2 1

To singles who care about spiritual growth
enough to do the hard work,
may God bless you in all you are doing and
make your dating especially fruitful
—H.C.

To all singles who want to make dating work God's way
—J.T.

CONTENTS

WHY YOU DON'T HAVE TO
KISS DATING GOOD-BYE

*D*r. Cloud, what is the biblical position on dating?" At first, I thought I had misheard the question. But the same question kept coming up around the country whenever I spoke to singles. We don't believe the Bible gives a position on dating. It's an activity a lot of people engage in, yet, as with a lot of other things, the Bible does not talk about it. What the Bible does talk about is being a loving, honest, growing person in whatever you do. So we would say that the biblical position on dating has much more to do with the person you are and are becoming than on whether or not you date. The biblical position on dating would be to date in a holy way.

This question about dating was asked in part in response to a movement that suggests all people should give up dating. We certainly understand the reasons behind the movement. Pain, disillusionment, and detrimental effects to one's spiritual life are three valid reasons for giving up on dating. But we don't think dating is the problem; we think people are. In the same way that cars don't kill people, but drunk drivers do, dating does not hurt people, but dating in out-of-control ways does.

The underlying issue is often the lack of appropriate structure within, among other things, a person's character, support system, values, and relationship with God. In other words, a lack of *boundaries*—and that is a character issue, a people problem. And the lack of appropriate structure, the lack of boundaries, is a maturity problem. So saying that dating is bad because people get hurt is a little like saying that because there are car accidents, no one should drive.

Avoiding dating isn't the way to cure the problems encountered in dating. The cure is the same as the Bible's cure for all of life's problems, and that is *spiritual growth leading to maturity*. Learning how to love, follow God, be honest and responsible, treat others as you want to be treated, develop self-control, and build a fulfilling life will ensure better dating.

We think dating can be a very good experience. Consider now a few of the benefits we see in dating:

1. Dating gives people the opportunity to learn about themselves, others, and relationships in a safe context.

2. Dating provides a context to work through issues.

3. Dating helps build relationship skills.

4. Dating can heal and repair.

5. Dating is relational and has value in and of itself.

6. Dating lets someone learn what he or she likes in the opposite sex.

7. Dating gives a context to learn sexual self-control and other delay of gratification.

Dating done poorly can lead to hurt and pain. Dating done well can lead to wonderful fruits in the life of the teen and the adult single. If you take this series seriously, seek God as deeply as you know how, establish a healthy community of friends to support you in the process, and keep God's boundaries for living a fulfilled but holy life, then dating can be something wonderful indeed.

For dating to be a great time of life, it must be balanced with God's boundaries of what is good. We hope *Boundaries in Dating* helps you find that safety, fulfillment, growth, and freedom.

There are many people who have been integral in the production of this material. We would like to thank Lisa Guest, especially, for all her diligent work and for the care she brings for God and the ones who use these materials. Lisa approaches our material with a deep sense of understanding and commitment to the finished work. Thanks also to Sealy Yates, our agent; the great staff of Zondervan; and the many singles whose feedback helped us in our thinking.

Henry Cloud, Ph.D.
John Townsend, Ph.D.

Session One

Why Boundaries in Dating?

OVERVIEW

In this session you will

- Consider patterns of unhealthy dating and benefits of healthy dating.

- Define what boundaries are—and why they are important.

- Find out what you are responsible for within your boundaries.

- Begin to see how boundaries function in a healthy dating relationship.

VIDEO SEGMENT

Dating: People Problems and Potential Benefits

- You probably don't need to kiss dating good-bye. Dating has its problems, but these problems point not to a problem with dating, but to a problem with people and their immaturity.

- Learning how to love, follow God, be honest and responsible, treat others as you would want to be treated, develop self-control, and build a fulfilling life will ensure better dating.

- Dr. Cloud and Dr. Townsend will address problems in dating by looking at the lack of appropriate structure within, among other things, a person's character, support system, values, and relationship with God. In other words, a lack of boundaries.

- Dating can be a great time of life, but it must be balanced with God's boundaries of what is good.

- If you take this series seriously, seek God as deeply as you know how, establish a healthy community of friends to support you in the process, and keep God's boundaries for living a fulfilled but holy life, then dating can be something wonderful indeed.

ON YOUR OWN
Benefits of Dating

DIRECTIONS

Take 10 minutes to begin answering the questions below and reflect on the benefits of dating you've already experienced or that you hope to experience.

1. Dating gives people the opportunity to learn about themselves, others, and relationships in a safe context.

   • What have you learned—or do you expect to learn—about yourself in a dating relationship?

   • What have you learned—or do you expect to learn—about other people from dating relationships?

   • What context makes dating "safe"? (Hint: community!)

2. Dating provides a context to work through issues.

   • When have you been surprised once you moved on from an initial impression and got to know better the person you were dating? Explain.

   • What have you learned—or do you expect to learn—from dating about what you value in a person for the long-term?

3. Dating helps build relationship skills.
   - What lack of certain relationship skills have you realized as you've dated? Consider communication, vulnerability, trust, assertiveness, honesty, self-sacrifice, and listening.

   - What, if anything, has dating helped you learn about relationship or about how you function in relationship?

4. Dating can heal and repair.
   - When have you seen or experienced for yourself dating as a place of learning, healing, and growth even if that relationship didn't lead to marriage?

   - Dating is a place where good things happen in people's souls. Name one or two good things that you've experienced—or hope to experience—in dating.

5. Dating is relational and has value in and of itself.
   - Why is relationship valuable? See, for instance, Genesis 2:18, Ecclesiastes 4:9–12, Galatians 6:2, and Hebrews 10:24–25.

- As you've dated, whom have you simply enjoyed getting to know even though the relationship didn't lead to marriage?

6. Dating lets someone learn what he or she likes in the opposite sex.
   - What we sometimes think we like is not what would really be good for us long-term, but we have to find this out. When have you seen this truth played out or perhaps experienced it yourself? Be specific about the lesson learned.

   - Dating enables people to find out what they like, what they need, what is good for them in another person, and what they did not like or need. What discoveries, if any, have you made in each of the following three categories thanks to your dating?

   What you like in another person

   What you need in another person

   What is good for you in another person

7. Dating gives a context to learn sexual self-control and other delays of gratification.
   - Why are sexual self-control and other delays of gratification essential in dating?

   - Why are sexual self-control and other delays of gratification essential in marriage?

VIDEO SEGMENT
Freedom, Responsibility, and Boundaries

- Many of the struggles people experience in dating are caused by some problem in the areas of freedom and responsibility. By freedom we mean your ability to make choices based on your values, rather than choosing out of fear, guilt, or need. By responsibility, we mean your ability to execute your tasks in keeping the relationship healthy and loving, as well as being able to say no to things for which you shouldn't be responsible.

- We believe that healthy boundaries are key to preserving freedom, responsibility, and, ultimately, love in your dating life.

- A boundary is a property line. Just as a physical fence marks where your yard ends and your neighbor's begins, a personal boundary distinguishes what is your emotional or personal property and what belongs to someone else. When another person tries to control you, tries to get too close to you, or asks you to do something you don't think is right, your boundary has been crossed.

- Boundaries serve two important functions. First, they define us. Boundaries show what we are and are not; what we agree and disagree with; what we love and hate.

- The second function of boundaries is that they protect us. Boundaries keep good things in and bad things out.

- Boundaries are fences protecting your property. In dating, your property is your own soul. You and only you are responsible for what's inside your boundaries—things like your love, your emotions, your values, your behaviors, and your attitudes.

LET'S TALK

Freedom and Responsibility

DIRECTIONS

1. Form groups of three or four people.

2. Answer the questions within your group, giving each person the opportunity to share.

3. Choose a representative to share your group's ideas after the exercise is over.

4. You will have 5 minutes for the first two questions and 5 minutes for the second two.

Freedom is your ability to make choices based on your values, rather than choosing out of fear, guilt, or need.

1. Think about some of the choices you've recently made, ideally in a dating relationship, but perhaps in a friendship or family relationship. To what degree did fear, guilt, or need motivate your choice? What did you fear, what were you feeling guilty about, what guilt were you trying to avoid, and/or what need were you trying to meet?

2. What problems can arise in a dating relationship if you're making choices out of fear, guilt, or need rather than based on your values? Give a real-life example or two.

Responsibility is your ability to execute your tasks in keeping the relationship healthy and loving, as well as being able to say no to things for which you shouldn't be responsible.

3. Again, think about a recent dating experience, a friendship, or a relationship with a family member. What have you done to keep the relationship healthy and loving? Be specific about one or two tasks. Also describe an opportunity you had to say no to something for which you shouldn't be responsible. Be specific about that something, then explain why you were or weren't able to say no. What were the consequences of your action or inaction?

4. What problems can arise in a dating relationship if you're not taking responsibility to speak the truth in love, to protect love by confronting problems (Ephesians 4:15)? Give a real-life example or two.

A FEW MORE THOUGHTS ON...
BOUNDARIES
What Boundaries Define and Protect

Boundaries are a fence protecting your property. In dating, your property is your own _____. Some of the contents of your soul—your self—that boundaries define and protect are:

- Your love: your deepest capacity to _____ and _____

- Your emotions: your need to _____ your feelings and not be _____ by someone else's feelings or behavior

- Your _____: your need to have your life reflect what you _____ about most deeply

- Your behaviors: your _____ over how you _____ in your dating relationship

- Your attitudes: your stances and _____ about _____ and your date

You and only you are _____ for what is inside your boundaries. If someone else is controlling your love, emotions, or values, they are not the problem. Your inability to _____ on their control is the problem.

A FEW MORE THOUGHTS ON...
BOUNDARIES

Tools and Tips for Using and Protecting Boundaries

Some tools available to you for setting limits and protecting your boundaries include:

- Words: telling someone _____ and being _____ about your disagreement

- The truth: bringing _____ to a problem

- Distance: allowing _____ or physical _____ between two people to protect or as a consequence for irresponsible behavior

- Other people: using supportive _____ to help keep a limit

- Consequences: _____ your limits in the relationship

Sometimes you will use boundaries to simply let your date know you better: "I am sensitive and wanted you to know that, so that we can be aware that I might get hurt easily." At other times, you may need to use boundaries to _____ a problem and _____ yourself or the relationship: "I will not go as far as you want physically, and if you continue pushing, I will not see you again." Either way, boundaries give you _____ and _____.

ON YOUR OWN
How Boundary Problems Show Themselves

DIRECTIONS

There are lots of ways dating suffers when freedom and responsibility are not appropriately present. Read through the points below, thinking about your patterns in relationships with family and friends as well as dates. Then, take a few moments to answer the questions. You will have 5 minutes to complete this exercise.

- **Loss of freedom to be oneself.** A person will give up her identity and lifestyle to keep a relationship together. Then, when her true feelings emerge, the other person doesn't like who she really is.

- **Being with the wrong person.** When our boundaries are unclear or undeveloped, we run the risk of allowing people inside who shouldn't be there.

- **Dating from inner hurt rather than from our values.** Often people with poor boundaries have some soul-work to do. So, instead of letting their values guide their choices, the hurt part inside them picks people to be in relationship with.

- **Not dating.** People withdraw to avoid hurt and risk.

- **Doing too much in the relationship.** Many people with boundary problems overstep their bounds and don't know when to stop giving of themselves.

- **Freedom without responsibility.** When one person enjoys the freedom of dating and takes no responsibility for himself or for developing the relationship, problems occur.

- **Control issues.** Sometimes the person more serious about the relationship attempts to rein in the other person by manipulation, guilt, domination, or intimidation. Love becomes secondary and control, primary.

- **Not taking responsibility to say no.** A person with this "nice guy" attitude allows disrespect and poor treatment by a date. The person disowns the responsibility to set a limit on bad things happening to him or her.

- **Sexual impropriety.** Couples avoid taking responsibility for maintaining appropriate physical limits, or one person is the only one with the "brakes," or they ignore the deeper issues that are driving the activity.

1. Where, if at all, do you see yourself in this list? Be honest with yourself so that you can learn and grow.

2. Where has someone you've dated fit one of these nine categories? How did that behavior impact the relationship?

Boundary Building

Before the next session, finish going through the questions in "Benefits of Dating." Then look around at your life and your relationships, dating and otherwise. Note below any situations in which you would have liked to have taken greater control of your time, energy, and resources. Also note those times when you experienced the freedom of doing what you wanted and of serving others in the ways you chose. In the first list, you will discover in what areas boundaries are needed; in the second, you will see where setting boundaries worked for you. The goal of this series is to help you build and maintain healthy, effective boundaries.

Suggested Reading

For more thoughts on this session's topic, read "Why Dating?" and "Why Boundaries in Dating?" the preface and chapter 1 of *Boundaries in Dating.* For a more thorough explanation of boundaries, look at chapters 1 and 2 in Dr. Cloud and Dr. Townsend's book *Boundaries: When to Say YES, When to Say NO to Take Control of Your Life.*

Session Two

Requiring and Embodying Truth

OVERVIEW

In this session you will

- Consider the truth that where there is deception, there is no relationship.

- Look at six deceptions common in the world of dating.

- Review your options when someone is not honest with you.

- Discover some reasons why people lie and learn what to do if you are lied to.

- Be called to live in the light of honesty.

VIDEO SEGMENT
Standing on Quicksand

- Where there is deception, there is no relationship.
- When you are with someone who is deceptive, you never know what reality is.
- There are many different ways to deceive someone in the world of dating:

1. Deception about your relationship
2. Deception about being friends
3. Deception about other people
4. Deception about who you are
5. Deception about facts
6. Deception about hurt and conflict

LET'S TALK

Deception in Dating

DIRECTIONS

1. The leader will be dividing the class into six groups and assigning each group one kind of deception to discuss.

2. Answer the questions listed for your group's type of deception, giving each person the opportunity to share.

3. Choose a representative from your small group to share your ideas after the exercise is over.

4. You'll have 5 minutes to complete this exercise.

Deception about Your Relationship

1. When, if ever, have you been deceived about a relationship's significance to the other person involved? What did you learn from your experience?

2. When, if ever, have you deceived a person you were dating about the relationship's significance to you? What did you learn from that experience or from this discussion of such an experience?

Deception about Being Friends

1. When, if ever, has someone pretended to be a friend to you but had ulterior motives? What impact did that deception have on the "friendship"?

2.   When, if ever, have you pretended to be a friend but had ulterior motives? What would have been a healthier (i.e., honest) approach?

Deception about Other People

1.   When, if ever, has someone you've dated been less than honest about someone in his or her life? What happened after that deception was revealed?

2.   When, if ever, have you been less than honest with someone about another person in your life? What statement of the truth could you have made early on? What pain (your own or someone else's) might have been avoided had you been honest?

Deception about Who You Are

1.   Why do you hesitate, if you do, to be honest about everything, from the kind of ice cream you like to what you believe about God? What does your answer tell you about yourself—and what will you do to become healthier?

2.   Maybe you've known or dated someone who wasn't able to be honest, who hesitated even to express an opinion or make a choice. How did you respond? Why is such behavior bad for a relationship?

Deception about Facts

1. When, if ever, has someone you've known or dated lied about reality? Was that deception a red flag for you? Why or why not? Why would such deception be a red flag?

2. When, if ever, have you lied about reality to someone you've known or dated? Why did you do that? What impact did your dishonesty have on your relationship? (Or, if you've never experienced this, what impact could this kind of dishonesty have on a relationship?) What are you doing to become a person of greater integrity?

Deception about Hurt and Conflict

1. When there is a problem with how you've been treated or when you have suffered some hurt, you must be honest. When have you opted for honesty? What happened? And when, if ever, have you kept quiet instead of being honest—and what happened in the relationship?

2. How do you respond when a person is honest about how you have hurt him or her or when you're trying to resolve a conflict? How would you like to respond—and what will you do to get to that point?

Being honest is totally up to you. What the person you are dating does you cannot control. But you can decide what kind of person you are going to be, and as a result, you will also be deciding what kind of person you are going to be with.

VIDEO SEGMENT

Honesty: The Best Boundary of All

- Where there is deception, there is no relationship.

- Why do people lie? Some people lie out of shame, guilt, fear of conflict or loss of love, or other fears. Other liars lie as a way of operating and deceive people for their own selfish ends.

- Spend your time and your heart on honest people. Have a zero-tolerance policy when it comes to deception. Lying should have no place in your life.

- If you don't want to be in relationship with a liar, be an honest person yourself—honest with yourself and honest with other people.

- Be light and attract light. That is the best boundary of all.

LET'S TALK

Truth or Consequences?

DIRECTIONS

Please form groups of three or four and discuss the questions below. Be sure to allow enough time so that each member of the group has an opportunity to share. You will have 10 minutes for this exercise.

1. Trying to help someone learn to tell the truth is a noble goal. But why is the attempt to rehabilitate not appropriate in a dating relationship? And why should you run, run, run from a perpetual liar?

2. Drs. Cloud and Townsend are clear, straightforward, and unwavering: *Do not tolerate lying,* period. Nevertheless, they understand that intimacy grows in a dating relationship, and that people use a "fig leaf" to cover up sometimes. Explain in practical terms how those points don't weaken their call to not tolerate lying.

3. Why does being honest attract honest people rather than deceivers? Feel free to use Jesus' metaphor of light and darkness in your answer (John 3:19–21).

A FEW MORE THOUGHTS ON . . .
DEALING WITH DECEPTION

Don't tolerate deception or lying when it happens. Make a rule: "I have to be with someone who is honest with me about what they are thinking or feeling." But what should you do if you are lied to? Here are six steps Dr. Cloud and Dr. Townsend suggest:

1.   _____ the lie.

2.   Hear the response and see how much _____ and _____ there is for the lying.

3.   Try to figure out what the lying _____ in the relationship. If the person is afraid, guilty, or fears the loss of your love, then work on that dynamic and try to determine if the character issue is changing. But be _____.

4.   Look at the level of _____ and _____. How significantly is the person pursuing _____ and _____? How internally _____ is he or she to get better?

5.   Is the change being _____? Make sure you give it enough _____. Just hearing "I'm sorry" is not good enough.

6.   Look at the kind of _____ it was. Was it to _____ himself or herself or just to serve _____ ends? If it is the latter, face reality squarely that you are with a person who loves himself more than the truth and face what that means. If the former, think long and hard, and have a good reason to continue in the relationship.

Honesty is the bedrock of any relationship. This week, be on the alert for moments when you're tempted, for whatever reason, to deceive. Make it your prayer to stand strong and be truthful. (If you notice a severe tendency to lie in order to deceive others for your own selfish ends, consider getting help.) Ask the Holy Spirit to help you be light.

Boundary Building

- Look again at "A Few More Thoughts on... Dealing with Deception." What steps listed there would be hard for you to take? Who could help you take those steps if you ever need to?
- Review why you should deal with lying in a relationship rather than ignoring it or pretending it isn't there.
- Are you an honest person? Explain why you've answered as you have. What evidence (including people you're in relationship with) can you point to in support of your yes or no?
- This week be on the alert for moments when you're tempted, for whatever reason, to deceive. Make it your prayer to stand strong and be truthful. (If you notice a severe tendency to lie in order to deceive others for your own selfish ends, consider getting help.) Ask the Holy Spirit to help you be light.

Suggested Reading

For more thoughts on this session's topic, read chapter 2 in *Boundaries in Dating:* "Require and Embody Truth." For a more thorough self-evaluation, look at chapter 2 in the *Boundaries in Dating Workbook.*

Session Three

Taking God on a Date

OVERVIEW

In this session you will

- Define and compare upside-down and right-side-up dating.

- Look at several aspects of your spiritual life that you will want to bring into a relationship.

- Learn how to evaluate the fruit of a dating relationship.

- Be encouraged to develop a relationship in which each person is challenging the other to "walk the talk."

VIDEO SEGMENT
Right-Side-Up Dating

- The issue is not how to fit our spiritual life into our dating life; rather, it is how to fit our dating life into our spiritual life. The right-side-up approach is to bring dating before God and ask for his guidance.

- Dependence on a date for the status of one's relationship with God can be a form of idolatry.

- When we demand that dating bring us the love, fulfillment, or desire we want without allowing God to point the way, we run the risk of going to the creation rather than the Creator as our ultimate source of life.

- Surrendering all of your life to God is the first and necessary step of bringing dating in line with God.

- Does your dating relationship bring you closer to God or push you further away? To evaluate the fruit of your dating relationship, ask yourself these questions:

Does the person challenge you spiritually, rather than you having to be the impetus?

Do you experience spiritual growth from interacting with that person?

Are you drawn to the transcendent God through that person?

Do you have an alliance with the other person in your spiritual walks?

Is the spiritual connection based on reality? Is the person authentic as well as spiritual?

Is the relationship a place of mutual vulnerability about weaknesses and sins?

LET'S TALK

Bringing Your Spiritual Life into a Dating Relationship

DIRECTIONS

1. Below you'll see five aspects of your life that you will want to bring into an open and spiritually healthy dating relationship. You'll also notice that one question in each section is italicized. Those are this week's "Boundary Building" exercise for you to do at home, so leave those alone for now.
2. You will be splitting up into five groups. The leader will be assigning each group one of these five aspects of life. Your group will have 8 minutes to read through your section and discuss the questions.
3. After the group is called back together, a spokesperson from each group will share their group's ideas with the rest of us.

FIVE ASPECTS OF LIFE

1. **Faith story.** Every believer has a story of how their relationship with God began and developed.
   Why is your faith story important to share?

   What elements of someone else's faith story (a date's, a friend's, or a relative's) have encouraged you and drawn you closer to that person and to the Lord?

   What faith story do you—or could you—share with a date?

2. **Values.** Your values are the architecture of who you are. They are comprised of what you believe is most important in life and how you conduct your life in accordance with these beliefs.

Why is each of the following values important to share with a date?

- Theology

- Finances

- Calling in life

- Family

- Relationships

- Sex

- Job and career

- Social issues

How do you or could you make each of the following values part of your dating world? What questions could you ask and what stances would you take?

- Theology

- Calling in life

- Relationships

- Job and career

- Finances

- Family

- Sex

- Social issues

3. **Struggles.** Failure, loss, confusion, mistakes, and learning experiences are part of the life of faith. To know a person's spiritual walk is also to know the times they stumbled in the darkness.

   Why is it important to share with a date such struggles as periods of being unsure about God's care or existence; living life apart from God; spiritual adolescence (challenging everything you've been taught); or times of self-absorption when you neglected your spiritual growth?

   When, if ever, has being brought into a date's or a friend's spiritual struggle made that relationship richer, if not easier? Explain.

   Which of your own spiritual struggles do you need to share at an appropriate time if you want to be known in a dating relationship? How would you describe or explain the issue(s)?

4. **Spiritual autonomy.** People who are trying to pull off a successful dating relationship need to know that the other person is spiritually autonomous. That is, he has his own walk with God that he pursues on a regular basis, regardless of his circumstances.

   Why is it important to date (and marry!) someone who is owning his or her spiritual walk? For starters, consider Ecclesiastes 4:10.

Why is time key to determining whether your date is truly spiritually autonomous?

Are you spiritually autonomous? If so, how would you deal with a date when it became obvious that the person and you were not spiritually autonomous? Or, if you and the person you are dating aren't spiritually autonomous, what steps will you take to get there? For instance, what spiritual discipline will you focus on? Be specific.

5. **Friendships.** You can learn a lot about people by the sort of friends they keep. The number of Christian friends they have, for instance, can be a telling detail.

Why is it important to know (not just know about) your date's friends?

Think of a friend or a date. What does that person's friendships reveal?

What do your friendships reveal about you, your priorities, your faith, your spiritual health?

These questions about a person's spiritual condition are not meant to be tools for judgmental scrutiny. Instead, they are intended to help both you and your date to examine your hearts and your relationships with God and each other.

VIDEO SEGMENT
Walking Your Talk

- Don't interpret religious agreement or passivity on your date's part as spiritual compatibility!

- It is important to be in agreement on the fundamentals of the Christian faith, but you also want to be in relationship with someone who has thought through their own spiritual issues deeply and individually and has reached their own conclusions.

- Fall in love with someone who is passionate about matters of faith, enough to wrestle with and discuss their meaning with you. Some of the most meaningful times of growth for dates can be when two people argue, read the Bible, and come to terms on spiritual matters.

- Watch to see how your date integrates faith into real life. Religious people *know* the Truth, but spiritual people *do* it.

- Be part of each other's spiritual growth and conduct. Even if you do not end up marrying each other, take the stance that during your tenure as dates, you both will grow spiritually.

- We encourage you to develop a relationship in which you are both challenging each other to "walk your talk."

- Evidence of walking your talk is found in the ability to love and be humble. Truly spiritual people know they don't "have it all together." In fact, the opposite is true: they know how deep their failings are and how much they need God's grace. As a result, they are able to empty themselves and love other people.

ON YOUR OWN
Spiritual Health and Growth

We will be doing this as an individual exercise. Work through the questions. (You might want to spend the most time on question 4.) You will have 10 minutes to do this exercise.

The design issue. The deepest part of you is made to desire spiritual intimacy with another person. If that part of you is working properly, you will seek out healthy spirituality in others.

1. What do your relationships (past and present, dating and otherwise) show about whether you are seeking out healthy spirituality in others?

Spiritual development path. Spiritual development means that you are not who you were nor are you who you will be.

2. What is good advice if a person's date is still questioning the content and meaning of Christianity?

Areas of belief and practice. As you get to know your date spiritually, you will need to decide what disagreements about belief and practice you can live with and which you can't.

3. What is a wise course of action if your date's beliefs or spiritual practices are a red flag?

Differences in spiritual level. Many people struggle with questions about dating others who are at a different level than they are spiritually.

4. In light of what you've learned in this session, what advice would you give the first party mentioned in each pair listed below?

    Christian who loves a non-Christian

    Committed Christian who is dating an uncommitted Christian

    Mature Christian who is getting serious about a new Christian

A FEW MORE THOUGHTS ON . . .
SPIRITUAL COMPATIBILITY AND DATING

Which of the following are issues for you? Make them a topic of both prayer and awareness.

- Wanting your date to be _____ spiritually

- Trying to _____ the other person spiritually

- Denying spiritual _____ in the relationship

- Missing our own spiritual _____ and focusing on our partner's

- Being afraid to address spiritual _____

Second, what are you currently doing to _____ in Christ and _____ his paths—or what could you be doing?

As we continue to grow in Christ, it becomes easier to love and invest our hearts wisely and well in our dating lives.

Boundary Building

Answer the italicized questions in "Bringing Your Spiritual Life into a Dating Relationship" so you can work on living out the lessons of this session.

Suggested Reading

For more thoughts on this session's topic, read chapter 3 in *Boundaries in Dating:* "Take God on a Date." For a more thorough self-evaluation, look at chapter 3 in the *Boundaries in Dating Workbook*.

Session Four
Setting Boundaries on Aloneness and on the Past

OVERVIEW

In this session you will

- Review seven signs of giving up healthy boundaries because of the fear of being alone.

- Learn why it is important to put a boundary around your wish for relationship—and how to do that.

- See what your past dating patterns show you about yourself.

VIDEO SEGMENT

A Boundary around Your Wish for Relationship

- Some people just can't stand being alone, and their fear of being alone keeps them from having boundaries with bad relationships.

- Dr. Cloud and Dr. Townsend offer these seven signs of giving up healthy boundaries because of the fear of being alone:

  1. Putting up with behavior that is disrespectful
  2. Giving in to things that are not in accord with your values
  3. Settling for less than you know you really desire or need
  4. Staying in a relationship that you know has passed its deadline
  5. Going back into a relationship that you know should be over
  6. Getting into a relationship that you know is not going anywhere
  7. Smothering the person you are dating with excessive needs or control

In cases like these, a peron's dating is ruled by their internal isolation, rather than by their God, goals, values, and spiritual commitments.

- To be happy in a relationship, and to pick the kind of relationship that is going to be the kind you desire, you must be able to be happy without one.

- In order to cure your fear of being alone, put a boundary around your wish for a relationship.

ON YOUR OWN

Curing the Fear of Being Alone

DIRECTIONS

Take 10 minutes to consider the points you find below.

In order to cure your fear of being alone, you need to put a boundary around your wish for a dating relationship. There is nothing wrong with the desire; just don't let it be a demand that controls you. Instead, deal with the nature of that wish and the fears involved. Cure that fear first, and then find a relationship. How do you cure that fear?

1. Strengthen your relationship with God. How will you do that? Make a list of some specific action steps you can take. Then circle the step you will take this week.

2. Strengthen your relationships with safe, healthy Christians. Who in your life falls into that category—or where will you find safe, healthy Christians?

3. Get a support system to ground you so that you can make dating choices out of strength, not out of weakness or dependency.

   • Describe your support system—or jot down some ideas about developing a stronger one.

- In those supportive relationships, are you allowing yourself
  to be appropriately dependent, have needs, and express
  pain and hurts? Support your answer with specific examples of your vulnerability.

4. A person living a full life of spiritual growth, personal growth,
   vocational growth, altruistic service, hobbies, and intellectual
   growth does not have the time or inclination to be dependent
   on a date. We've already addressed your spiritual life. What
   are you doing to be active and grow in these other areas?

Personal development

Job/career

Service to others

Hobbies and recreation

Intellectual pursuits

5. In addition to having an active life, work on the issues in your
    soul. What issues (past childhood hurts, recurring themes and
    patterns in your relationships and work life, other areas of
    brokenness, pain, and dysfunction) are you or could you be
    addressing? Is a fear of aloneness related to any of these soul
    issues?

The best boundary against giving in to bad relationships, less-
than-satisfactory relationships, or bad dynamics in a good relationship is your not being dependent on that relationship. And
that is going to come from being grounded in God, grounded in a
support system, working out your issues, having a full life, and
pursuing wholeness. If you are doing those things, you will be less
subject to saying yes when you should be saying no.

VIDEO SEGMENT

A Boundary with Your Past

- Begin to evaluate your dating past. Did you date too seriously? Was it difficult for you to be honest? Did you neglect friendships? Did your life revolve around dating instead of your dating being part of a balanced life? When you recognize patterns like these, you can begin to work through them.

- Your past can provide a great deal of necessary information on what to do and what to avoid in dating, either through the satisfaction of doing it right, or the pain of doing it wrong.

- To blithely skip over the past is to ignore important aspects of reality, while to pay attention to what you have done before is to take ownership of your present and future.

- The first dating problem is denying that your past demonstrates a problem!

- Understanding our past helps us grow.

- Be afraid of your past: have a healthy fear of the consequences of repeating the past.

- Ask your buddies or girlfriends, God, and yourself the same question: What can I learn from my dating past that will help me avoid bad things or experience good things in the future?

A FEW MORE THOUGHTS ON ...
A HEALTHY FEAR OF THE PAST

- Be afraid of _____ your present relationship. Don't neglect your past just because your present is good. Doing the hard work of growth now can help prevent problems in the future.

- Be afraid of _____ with your present relationship.

- Be afraid of being _____. Perhaps in the past you have invested in and trusted someone who was not very trustworthy. Look at that past: Consider why you have been hurt along the way.

- Be afraid of _____.

- Be afraid of reducing your _____. People who haven't learned lessons from the past are less free to be themselves, grow, and make decisions.

- We need to clearly understand both the prospects we face if things remain the same as well as the risks of not learning and growing from our past. This two-fold understanding helps us bear the pain of changing.

LET'S TALK

Why the Past Still Rules

DIRECTIONS

1. The leader will be dividing you into four groups and assigning each group one of the four deterrents to working through and overcoming past dating patterns.

2. Read through and discuss the questions assigned to your group, making sure that each person gets a chance to share.

3. Choose a representative to share your group's ideas with the large group after the exercise is over.

4. You will have 5 minutes to answer your group's questions.

Lack of maturity. One indicator of character maturity is the ability to be aware, curious, and concerned about one's past patterns.

1. What evidence in a person's life would suggest that she is more interested in living only in the present than in learning from the past and growing for the future?

2. What can safe individuals do to help someone grow in love and truth?

Fear of the unknown. Fearing the unknown—worrying about what might happen if you change—can stall the growth process.

1. Which do many, if not most, people prefer: a known bad thing or an unknown thing? Why?

2. When being honest in a dating relationship is an unknown thing for a person, what can close friends do to help so that the unknown of honesty can become a known good thing?

Fear of the known. Some people repeat the past because they have tried to change their patterns and suffered greatly for some reason. The pain was sufficient to stop their attempt to change.

1. When can attempts to change and grow result in pain?

2. As the old Alcoholics Anonymous saying goes, change occurs when the pain of remaining the same is greater than the pain of changing. What pain, if any, are you living with in a current relationship? What pain of changing seems worse than that pain?

Isolation. One major obstacle to resolving the past is the state of being cut off from the source of life, which is relationship with God and others. Relationship is the fuel which makes change and growth possible.

1. When, if ever, have you experienced the comfort, support, or reality of relationship? Be specific. How did you benefit?

2. If a person doesn't have enough support to deal with the past and resolve it, to make change and growth possible, where can he or she go for fuel?

Boundary Building

During the week, work some more on the exercise "Why the Past Still Rules." Focus on the three deterrents to learning from past dating that your small group did not cover. Be sure to ask the questions of yourself as if you're the someone being referred to. That way you can learn from your past so that you don't repeat it. Also take some time to consider whether you are hoping that relationships will numb the ache that comes with being alone.

Suggested Reading

For more thoughts on this session's topic, read chapters 4 and 5 in *Boundaries in Dating:* "Dating Won't Cure a Lonely Heart" and "Don't Repeat the Past." For a more thorough self-evaluation, look at chapters 4 and 5 in the *Boundaries in Dating Workbook.*

Session Five

Whom Should I Be Dating? Part 1

OVERVIEW

In this session you will

- Look at both your preferences and your requirements for the people you date.

- Consider whether those preferences and requirements are too limiting or not limiting enough.

- Learn some reasons why opposites attract—and why those connections can be unhealthy.

VIDEO SEGMENT

What You Can—and Can't—Live With

- What do you look for in a person to date seriously or marry? You could probably list a few things without any hesitation.

- Some traits (being athletic, intellectual, or witty, for instance) are differences in taste.

- Other traits have nothing to do with tastes and natural differences. These traits have to do with *character*. You are initially attracted to a person's outsides, but over time you'll experience their insides as well.

- Look at your "boundaries of choices"—your requirements for the people you date. Ask yourself:

   Are your preferences too limiting? Do you need to be more open?

   Are some preferences more important than you realize? Value them!

   Which imperfections in a person's character are minor? You'll need to learn to deal with them.

   Which imperfections in a person's character are major? These are totally off-limits. You should never have to live with them.

- You are always going to be dating someone with flaws. But, remember, there are flaws you can live with, and those you can't.

- Be open to casually dating anyone of good character. If the person is of good character, go out and have a good time.

A FEW MORE THOUGHTS ON ...
PREFERENCES
Unhealthy Preferences

- Fears of _____ can attract you to detached people.

- Fears of autonomy can attract you to _____ people.

- Fears of being real can attract you to _____ people.

- Fears of your own _____ can attract you to "bad" people.

- Fears of your own _____ can attract you to weak, passive people.

- Unresolved family of origin issues can attract you to someone who is like a _____ you had trouble with.

Good Preferences

- *Common interests* help you determine how you spend your _____.

- *Common goals* determine how you spend your _____.

- *Common values* determine what _____ _____ you look for in a person.

ON YOUR OWN
Minor Imperfections

DIRECTIONS

On your own, read through and answer the questions found below. You will have 8 minutes to complete this exercise.

No one is perfect. Every person you date will be a person who will sin and let you down. However, as you evaluate the people you date, remember a few things.

1. You can live with sinners who have the ability to see when they have wronged you, to confess it, to care about how they have hurt you, and to work hard not to continue in that pattern. Which of these four areas do you need to work on so you can be a sinner people can live with?

2. The following traits suggest that a person is able to work on their imperfections:

    A relationship with God

    Ability to see where one is wrong

    Ability to be honest

    Ability to see the effects of the wrong on the other person

    Ability to empathize with those effects and be truly sorry for the other person as opposed to just feeling guilty

    Motivation to repent and change

    Ability to sustain repentance and change

    Commitment to a path of growth, a system of growth, and the involvement of other people in the growth process

    Ability to receive and utilize forgiveness

Why is such a person who meets these criteria a good bet? And which traits do you need to develop?

3. A person of good character will still fail, but generally they have "yellow light" sins that you can live with—as long as the person sees these problems in himself or herself and deals with them. Look below at the list of things that will annoy you but won't kill you, things you could learn to accept in mild doses. Which areas can you work on in yourself?

   Disorganization

   Difficulty with opening up and being direct about feelings or hurts

   Tendencies toward performance orientation

   Tendencies toward wanting to appear strong and avoiding vulnerability

   Perfectionism

   Some attempts to control

   Avoidance of closeness

   Impatience

   Messiness

   Nagging

4. What do these items listed suggest to you about where you could grow in being accepting and supportive of a fellow sinner? Put differently, what do you see about your tendency to be judgmental or perfectionistic?

None of us gets everything right in relationships, and as a result we all are somewhat of a pain to be with at times. That is normal. Also, since you have to date sinners, decide which sins you can live with, or at least work with.

LET'S TALK
Major Imperfections

DIRECTIONS

Pair up with a person near you and read through the questions found below. You will have 10 minutes to complete this exercise.

1. Character begins with yourself. In Psalm 101:2–8, David lists things he decided to avoid: faithlessness, perversity, evil, slander, pride, deceit, and wickedness. What can we do to build character in ourselves, godly character that is devoid of the traits David listed? What are *you* doing to build godly character?

2. Consider now some *personal* traits that are destructive to relationships.

Destructive Personal Traits

Acts like he has it all together instead of admitting weakness and imperfection

Is religious instead of spiritual

Is defensive instead of open to feedback

Is self-righteous instead of humble

Apologizes instead of changes

Avoids working on problems

Demands trust instead of proving himself trustworthy

Lies instead of telling the truth

Is stagnant and not growing

Is an addict

Is duplicitous

When have you seen someone hurt (or been hurt yourself) by someone acting out one or more of these traits?

Which traits listed point out areas in which you could be growing?

3. Consider the following *interpersonal* traits that are destructive to relationships:

   ### *Destructive Interpersonal Traits*

   Avoids closeness

   Thinks only about himself instead of the relationship and the other person

   Is controlling and resists freedom (in dating, this includes not respecting your limits in the physical realm)

   Flatters

   Condemns

   Plays "one up" or acts parental

   Is unstable over time

   Is a negative influence

   Gossips

   Is overly jealous and suspicious

   Negates pain

   Is overly angry

   When have you seen someone hurt (or been hurt yourself) by someone acting on one or more of these traits?

Which traits listed are areas in which you could be growing?

4. There are four steps to take if you find yourself in a dating relationship with someone who has a pattern of these destructive personal and/or interpersonal traits. They are the same as the steps to take if your date is not being truthful.

   1. Confront the problem directly.
   2. See what kind of response you get.
   3. Watch for a pattern of sustained repentance, change, and follow-through in growth.
   4. Only trust again and keep going if these "red lights" are no longer problems.

   Why would a support system be helpful, if not crucial, for someone needing to take these steps?

   Who in your support system can help you stand strong if and when you need to take these steps?

VIDEO SEGMENT

Beware When Opposites Attract

- The idea of complementary gifts and strengths is good for us emotionally, in more than one way. We have to learn humility to ask people for what we don't possess, and that helps us grow. We also can grow from the competencies of others.

- We should use and appreciate the abilities of those who have what we don't. However, the danger occurs when we make opposing styles or abilities a *basis* for relationship.

- Opposite-driven relationships often confuse dependency with true love.

- In mature couples, opposite traits are simply not a major issue. The two people are not drawn to opposite traits due to their own deficits; they are drawn to the values they share, such as love, responsibility, forgiveness, honesty, and spirituality.

- Attraction based on values is much more mature than attraction based on what you don't have inside.

- Immature couples seem to struggle more with finding someone who possesses the nurturance, structure, competence, or personality that they don't. Ultimately, they are looking for a parent to take care of part of them that they aren't taking care of in themselves.

- Make oppositeness a nonissue. Look more for character, love, and values than for which one of you has which qualities.

LET'S TALK
Why Opposites Attract

DIRECTIONS

Form groups of three or four and discuss the questions below. The italicized questions are for you to consider on your own as part of this week's "Boundary Building" exercise. Please disregard those at this time. You will have 10 minutes to complete this exercise.

What is it about their opposites that people find so attractive? Why are we attracted to our opposite? There are several answers to this question.

We do not want to work at developing ourselves. The essence of the opposite issue is not really about the other person. It is about using another person to avoid dealing with our own souls.

1. Why is this an unhealthy motive for dating?

2. *When have you or someone you know piggybacked on another person's strengths instead of addressing an area of growth that needed work?*

We want to be complete. We are drawn to those who possess what we do not, so that we can internalize and own that trait for ourselves.

3. Why is dating not a good arena in which to develop oneself in a specific and important aspect of growth?

4. *When has a mentor, teacher, counselor, or friend helped you develop a character trait? Be specific about the process and how you benefited.*

We are afraid of dealing with our deficits. Another reason opposites attract is our fear of looking at our own character flaws. Self-exploration and change can be scary.

5. How might the following fears play themselves out in dating—making mistakes and failing; risking making others angry; having others leave us; guilt over hurting others; reexperiencing a painful past; looking at parts of ourselves that we don't like to see?

6. *Which of these have been or are issues for you? How, if at all, have those fears played themselves out in your dating life?*

7. *What role can a support group or a safe friend play in helping you deal with your fear?*

We are spiritually lazy. It is simply easier to have others do for us what we don't want to do for ourselves. This is the nature of immaturity, or "spiritual laziness." Such immaturity is the rageaholic who has to have his girlfriend soothe him when he is angry rather than learning to self-soothe and deal with his rage. The impulsive shopper depends on her boyfriend to untangle her finances. The introverted man looks to his girlfriend to maintain the relationships he should be developing.

8. These examples of immaturity show people failing to take ownership for what they lack and continuing to demand that others provide it. Which scenario, if any, have you seen or lived out yourself?

9. *Whether the problem is fear or laziness, we need to deal with our own deficits instead of looking to a date to heal them.*

Session Six

Whom Should I Be Dating? Part 2

OVERVIEW

In this session you will

- Recognize the pointlessness and potential pain of falling in love with someone you wouldn't be friends with.
- Learn what to do if falling in love with someone you wouldn't be friends with is your pattern.
- Be warned against romanticizing a friendship.
- Discover various causes of such romanticization.
- Explore your loneliness to see if it is the normal need for connectedness or a sign of an injury that needs to be healed.

VIDEO SEGMENT

Don't Fall in Love with Someone You Wouldn't Be Friends With

- Many singles fall in love with someone they wouldn't be friends with. Perhaps you do too.

- If you are attracted to someone who does not possess the character and friendship qualities you need in a long-term relationship, do not think you are going to change him or her. If this is your pattern, see it as a problem, not simply a matter of not yet having found "the right one."

- Do everything possible to get to know the person you're attracted to. Can you share all of your values? Is the spiritual commitment the same? Are there character traits you find yourself ignoring, denying, or excusing? In short, would you pick this person as a friend?

- Are you confusing longing for being "in love"? Are you confusing infatuation with love?

- Find an accountability system to hold you to the boundary of not letting yourself go too far into a relationship with someone you would not be friends with. Say no to letting your heart get involved with a person whom you would not choose as a friend.

- The best boundary that you can have in your dating life is to begin every relationship with an eye toward friendship.

ON YOUR OWN
Reasons for Unhealthy Attraction

DIRECTIONS

Answer the questions below. (What you don't finish will be part of this week's "Boundary Building" exercise.) You will have 10 minutes for this exercise.

Unresolved family-of-origin issues. If you had problems in the family you grew up in, those problems may surface in your dating relationships. One woman was attracted to a person who was like a parent she had struggled with. Another was attracted to someone who was the diametrical opposite of the hurtful parent.

1. What unresolved family-of-origin issues, if any, might surface in your dating relationships? What could you do to resolve those issues before they interfere?

Unintegrated parts of yourself. Another prime reason you may be attracted to people who would not be good for you is that you are looking to resolve some aspect of yourself you have never faced. Often if you do not possess a certain quality, you are drawn to someone who possesses it in the extreme. Sometimes a person is attracted to a bad thing: a "saint" falls head over heals with a "sinner." And sometimes a person has a pain or hurt she has never faced and is drawn to someone who has a lot of pain and problems.

2. When, if ever, have you seen or perhaps experienced for yourself one of these three scenarios? Whatever is in your heart is what you are going to find yourself dealing with, in one way or another, as you date. What can you do to guard your heart (Proverbs 4:23) and make it healthy so you will not be attracted to the wrong kinds of people?

Defensive hope. Have you had a lot of disappointment and loss in your life? If so, it may be difficult for you to let go of things, even things that are not good. You may have developed a pattern of "defensive hope": your hope that a date will change is a defense against the loss that would come with letting go of the relationship.

3. If you've ever been in this kind of situation, describe that experience and what you were thinking and feeling as you chose to stay in the unhealthy relationship. What would you say to someone in a similar situation today? What might help that person realize that the grief of letting go would not swallow him up?

Romanticizing. A "hopeless romantic" may be vulnerable to charmers who don't have the underlying character to carry on a lasting relationship. "Charm is deceptive" (Proverbs 31:30), and charmers and their prey are unable to get past romanticizing to real intimacy. If you have a tendency to romanticize everything, then you are avoiding the reality of what is going on. And the reality is what you are going to have to live with.

4. Do you describe yourself as a "hopeless romantic"? Do you have a long-standing Cinderella complex ("Someday my prince will come")? (Men can also have similar romantic feelings to the Cinderella complex.) Or are your fantasies a defense against depression or other kinds of disappointments? What can you do or who can you talk to to get a handle on what your romanticism is all about?

Undeveloped intimacy. Some people have never been connected with and known at a very deep level. At the most vulnerable parts of their heart, they have never been related to, so they don't know what real connection and intimacy is.

5. Are you aware of your undeveloped ability to be intimate? Does your dating history suggest that your detachment has been drawn to detachment? If you answer yes to either of these questions, what step toward a cure will you make? Specifically, what healing relationships—that are not romantic in nature—will you invest in so that all of your parts can be related to and find connection?

LET'S TALK
The Path of Friendship

CHARACTERISTICS OF A FRIEND

_____

_____

_____

_____

_____

_____

DIRECTIONS

Pair up with a person near you and answer the questions found below. You will have 6 minutes to do this exercise.

1. Think about lasting relationships you know of. What evidence do you see that each is built on friendship first?

2. The best boundary you can have in your dating life is to begin every relationship with an eye toward friendship. What does this advice mean in terms of what you do with a person in the early stages of a relationship? Put differently, what kinds of activities would help you see whether that person could be a friend?

3. Why should people not believe their feelings in the early stages of a possible dating relationship?

VIDEO SEGMENT

Don't Ruin a Friendship out of Loneliness

- Much good can come from healthy opposite-sex relationships, and much grief can be spared by not pursuing a romantic relationship when the feelings are simply not there.

- "Romanticizing a friendship" refers to making friends into something they are not.

- Romantic feelings come from an idealization of the other person.

- In a new relationship, each person knows little about the other person. Idealization fills in the gaps with good things in order to keep the couple involved in the relationship, and helps them tolerate the early parts of the developing connection.

- In a mature relationship, romantic idealization waxes and wanes. It arises out of a deep appreciation and gratitude for the person's presence and love, yet it retains the reality of who he or she is at the same time.

- In a struggling relationship, one person can develop romantic feelings for the other out of his or her own neediness. This neediness becomes "romanticized"; that is, it disguises its true nature in romance. This kind of romanticization is driven by loneliness, by a chronic, longstanding sense of emptiness in life, no matter what the circumstances.

- This loneliness is an indication that something is broken in one's soul, and needs to be repaired by God's healing process, not by a friendship-turned-romantic.

LET'S TALK

What Causes Romanticizing?

DIRECTIONS

1. Form groups of three or four.

2. Answer the questions found below.

3. The questions in italics will be part of this week's "Boundary Building" exercise. Please disregard them for now.

4. You will have 10 minutes for this exercise.

Conflicts in experiencing dependency. People who romanticize often are unable to feel their dependency for what it is: dependency. Fear of the depth of the internal emptiness; feeling bad as well as lonely; being ashamed of feeling needy; afraid to risk reaching out for fear of being hurt; feeling helpless and powerless when they feel their needs—these are some reasons people are unable to feel their dependency.

1. What are some healthy responses to feeling lonely? To feeling dependent or needy?

2. *Are you unable to feel your dependency as dependency? If so, which, if any, of the five reasons listed may be behind that inability?*

Failures in relating to the same sex. Often, those who romanticize their friends have a history of not being able to safely and deeply connect to the same sex so they keep trying to have significant connection with members of the opposite sex.

3. Romanticizers have pre-adult needs such as the need for belonging, for being safe, and for feeling comforted and

loved. What can a person do to let God and safe nonromantic relationships meet those needs?

4. *Where, if at all, do you see yourself limited in your ability to connect with members of the same sex? Are you, for instance, worried that you will hurt the other person, do you doubt that they have anything to offer, do you have contempt for the stereotypical weaknesses of their gender, or do you fear that you will lose opposite-sex opportunities by spending time with same-sex friends? What will you do about any truth you realize about yourself here?*

Idealizing romance. Some people think that romance is the highest form of friendship. Many people who are "into" romance feel that friendship is a grade lower than a romance. Don't get caught in the idea that you are missing out by keeping your friend as "only" your friend.

5. Romantic relationships are not better than friendships. They are different and meet different needs. List some of the differences and some of the different needs that are met.

6. *When, if ever, have you thought that a romantic relationship is better than a friendship and tried to elevate the friendship? What happened to the friendship—and what did you learn from the experience?*

Rescue/caretaking roles. Sometimes people who get caught up in romanticizing have tendencies to get into certain ways of relating called *rescuing* and *caretaking*. The "rescuee" will signal a need for someone to take care of him. The "caretaker" will receive the signal and go support, comfort, or solve the problems of the rescuee.

7. Why is this an unhealthy dynamic in a dating relationship?

8. *When, if ever, have you fallen first into this pattern and then fallen in love with either your caretaker or the one you cared for?*

Impulsiveness. Some people struggle with romanticization because they have difficulty with their drives and impulses. They become sexually involved very quickly, or are into quick, intense, "deep" connections.

9. Why doesn't impulsive romanticization lead to satisfying relationships?

10. *When, if ever, have you or someone you know tried to take either of these shortcuts to a significant relationship? What happened?*

A FEW MORE THOUGHTS ON ...
HOW TO KNOW A FRIENDSHIP FROM A ROMANCE

- Get connected _____ of the relationship.

- Evaluate the _____ of the relationship. True romance and a romanticized friendship are after very different goals.

- Get _____.

Healthy Romance	Romanticized Friendship
Desire is based on first being rooted in love elsewhere.	Desire is based on empty _____ for the other person.
Other's _____ is valued.	Other's freedom is a problem.
Relationship _____ friends.	Relationship shuts others out.
Conflicts work out okay.	Conflicts _____ the relationship.
_____ feelings.	One person feels romantic; the other doesn't.
Friendship and romantic feelings _____.	All-friend or all-romantic feelings; can't be both at the same time.

Boundary Building

This week, as you continue to think about whom you should be dating, finish "Reasons for Unhealthy Attraction," complete the italicized questions in "What Causes Romanticizing," and take time to use the "Healthy Romance/Romanticized Friendship" chart on page 83 to evaluate any current relationship you're wondering about.

Suggested Reading

For more thoughts on this session's topic, read chapters 7 and 8 in *Boundaries in Dating*: "Don't Fall in Love with Someone You Wouldn't Be Friends With" and "Don't Ruin a Friendship out of Loneliness." For a more thorough self-evaluation, look at chapters 7 and 8 in the *Boundaries in Dating Workbook*.

Session Seven

Solving Dating Problems When You're Part of the Problem, Part 1

OVERVIEW

In this session you will

- Consider the consequences of adapting to your date's wishes, needs, and desires rather than also being honest about your own.

- Think about what, if anything, keeps you from being honest about who you are.

- Learn both the value of moving slowly in a dating relationship and some signs of moving too fast.

- Look at why you may move too fast in a dating relationship.

85

VIDEO SEGMENT

Adapt Now, Pay Later

- It's better to find out early in a relationship that you are with someone who cannot adapt to your wishes than to find out much later or, God forbid, after marriage.

- Don't be someone you are not just to gain a person's love. If you do, the person is not loving you, but the role you are playing.

- You cannot go through life without also pursuing your own wishes, needs, and desires—nor should you. Your needs and desires are going to come out, and you had better find out early in the relationship how the person you are dating will deal with sometimes having to adapt to you.

- Be yourself from the beginning. If you are a real person from the start, a relationship of mutuality has a chance of developing. If you are not, then you might be headed for trouble.

ON YOUR OWN

Wishes, Needs, Desires

DIRECTIONS

Work through the following questions. You will have 10 minutes to complete this exercise.

An important lesson of this session is to *be yourself from the beginning,* and then you can find someone who is authentic as well.

1. What, if anything, keeps you from being yourself? What fears, past hurts, or daunting risks prompt you to be more compliant than may be healthy and wise?

2. Keri's friend Sandy helped her see reality and cope with the loss of Steve. What safe friend is close enough to see the dynamics of your dating relationship and whether you are really being yourself?

People who are selfish and controlling can only be that way if they are in relationship with someone who is adaptive. If someone stands up to them and is honest about his or her wants and desires, then the controlling person has to learn to share or gets frustrated and goes away.

3. If you tend to be adaptive, what is fueling that tendency and what can you do to heal the underlying hurt or meet the hidden need in a healthier way?

4. Similarly, what may be keeping you from being honest about wants and desires? And, again, what can you do to heal the underlying hurt or meet the hidden need in a healthier way?

A relationship between two authentic people has mutuality and partnership. It has give and take. It has equality. It has sharing and mutual self-sacrifice for the sake of the other and the relationship. If you are a real person from the start, a relationship of mutuality has a chance of developing.

VIDEO SEGMENT
Too Much, Too Fast

- The problem of premature commitment and overinvolvement in a dating relationship ("too much, too fast") is a common one.

- Dating for a year, not including the engagement period, is a good minimum. When you date for at least a year, you experience the rhythm of life and a wide variety of experiences, including holidays, fiscal periods, vacations, and school terms. You can see how the relationship weathers the flow of both people's lives.

- Many things, including loneliness, difficulty in leaving home, difficulties in sustaining friendships, and perfectionism, contribute to couples seeing time as an adversary.

- If your dating relationships tend to move too quickly, consider that a signal and ask yourself why. Make sure you're not moving quickly because you are avoiding some other pain, such as loneliness or inner hurt.

- Real love takes time and has no shortcut, but it is worth it. Ask God to make you patient with the process of love so that you will be able to experience its growth day by day.

LET'S TALK
Why Wait?

DIRECTIONS

1. The leader will divide you into three groups and assign each group one topic from below.
2. Each group should choose a spokesperson.
3. You will have 10 minutes to go through your group's topic. As before, the italicized questions are for you to answer at home as part of your "Boundary Building" exercise.
4. When the group is called back together, each group's spokesperson will be asked to share their group's thoughts.

Why should you wait, take time, and gradually become closer to a person to whom you are enormously attracted? Here are three answers to that question.

1. **Relationships do not tolerate shortcuts.** We have to understand the nature of relationships as God designed them. Relationships grow in a healthy manner only as they undergo experiences—and there is no shortcut to experiences. Consider these eight time-consuming dating activities:
   • Having enough talks to safely open up with each other
   • Entering each other's worlds of work, hobbies, worship, and service
   • Meeting and spending time with each other's friends
   • Understanding each other's strengths and weaknesses
   • Going over basic values and what is important in life to each other
   • Getting to know each other's families
   • Spending time away from each other to think through the relationship, both alone and with friends
   • Learning your best style of disagreement and conflict management

What is the value of each of these experiences? Why aren't shortcuts possible? (Could all this be done in a few short months?)

When have you been surprised by who a person (friend, business associate, or date) really was once you got to know that person through shared experiences? Comment on what the shared experiences revealed that you hadn't known about that person before.

2. **A measure of importance.** The time involved in dating someone should reflect the significance of the relationship. Simply put, the more important a decision is, the more time it should take to make it. Our most important human relationship should warrant the time due it.

   Read through the following list of some of the significant aspects of marriage:

   • A lifelong commitment to loving one person only
   • Forsaking all other opportunities for romantic love
   • Being in relationship with all the bad, immature, and broken parts of that person
   • Having your own bad, immature, and broken parts open to the scrutiny of that person
   • Solving conflict in ways that do not involve leaving the relationship
   • Staying in the relationship even if the other person changes for the worse
   • Being called to sacrifice many individual preferences for the sake of the relationship

Which of those serve as a wake-up call to the seriousness of marriage? What do these items suggest about the importance of not rushing the dating relationship?

When, if ever, have you experienced loneliness within a relationship? How did that compare to being alone?

3. **The nature of love.** Another reason to take your time is that this is a necessary part of learning how to love. Dating should not only produce a mate; it should also develop within you the ability to love that mate deeply and well. And love, as the Bible defines it, is a stance of working for the best for another person.

   Taking time in your dating relationship helps you clarify the distinction between need and love. What relationship have you've seen or perhaps been involved in that seemed propelled forward by one or more of needs listed below? Describe what happened.

   • Needing the security of knowing he has your total commitment

   • Wanting to end the sexual frustration that comes with singleness

   • Needing the relationship in order to feel complete

   • Needing someone to relate to in his life

   When has a friendship or dating relationship taught you something about how to love? Explain.

A FEW MORE THOUGHTS ON ... GOING TOO FAST

You Are Committing Too Quickly If ...

- You "know" each other _____ more than you "know" each other _____.

- You find yourself more _____ in the relationship than in areas of your life that are important to you.

- You abruptly _____ dating others.

- You get _____ from _____ that this seems to be going quickly.

Slowing Down the Pace

- _____ what is driving the pace (loneliness, fear of being out in the world, problems in making friends, or perfectionism). Work on those issues.

- Get a _____. A full life is probably the best antidote for getting too close, too fast. Ask God to help you get involved in real life: spending time on friends, work, hobbies, church, service, and God himself.

- Deliberately slow the pace to _____ the relationship. If the relationship is mature, it will withstand the test of slowing down.

- Investigate _____ is contributing to the pace. Does it tend to be _____, those you date, or both?

- Ask friends for _____. Humbly go to mature, safe friends and ask them to tell you when you're getting weird. Give them permission to tell you to _____!

Boundary Building

When, if ever, have you done more than the normal initial adapting in order not to jeopardize a developing relationship? When—and how—did you realize that things went smoothly only as long as you adapted to your date and that your date was unable to deal with your needs and desires?

Are you adapting now, only to pay later? Find out by evaluating yourself according to the following criteria:

1. Do you tell the truth about where you want to go and not go, or what you want to do or not do?
2. Are you honest about your preferences and desires?
3. Are you acting as if you like things that your date likes just so you will be accepted? Being liked for who you are requires that you be that person!
4. Are you afraid to share your desires and wants for fear of conflict?
5. Are you getting feedback from honest friends to see if you are really being yourself and if you are seeing the relationship realistically?

What do your answers tell you about whether you are adapting too much—and what are you going to do in light of what you've realized about yourself?

Also during the coming week, take some time to answer the italicized questions from the "Why Wait?" section and review the tips for slowing down a relationship found in "A Few More Thoughts on ... Going Too Fast." What do you need to do, if anything, to slow down the pace of your dating relationships?

Suggested Reading

For more thoughts on this session's topic, read chapters 10 and 11 in *Boundaries in Dating:* "Adapt Now, Pay Later" and "Too Much, Too Fast." For a more thorough self-evaluation, look at chapters 10 and 11 in the *Boundaries in Dating Workbook*.

Solving Dating Problems When You're Part of the Problem, Part 2

OVERVIEW

In this session you will

- Learn what it means to be kidnapped in a dating relationship and how to avoid it.

- Discover basic elements of safe dating so you can avoid being kidnapped.

- Look at the difference between false hope and merited hope, and when it is futile to hope a date will change.

- Define good blame and bad blame, consider whether you tend to blame rather than take responsibility, and learn how to put boundaries on the blame game.

VIDEO SEGMENT

Don't Get Kidnapped

- A relationship that gets rid of one's individual life and friends, time, and space is not a healthy relationship.

- Friends are an important space-giving freedom that will help you be healthier and more well-rounded. In addition, friends will notice if you are losing them to a dating relationship— and they'll let you know!

- Work out your dating relationship with the help of your friends. Spend time and energy with your dates, but then return to your community.

- One aspect of safe dating is to remain connected to your friends and support system. By doing so, you'll make sure that you are not vulnerable to what you cannot see on your own but would be able to see with the help of other people.

- Stay connected, stay safe, and stay wise.

ON YOUR OWN
Safe Dating

DIRECTIONS

On your own, please read the information and answer the questions found below. You will have 10 minutes to complete this exercise.

Friends provide a feedback base to see reality. The very state of being in love is a state of idealization, where the other person is not being viewed through the eyes of reality. We often can't see this idealization or the fact that we're becoming some-one other than who we really are, but hopefully our friends can.

1. What chunks of reality about a person you've been in love with have you not seen? What helped you finally see them?

2. What role did friends play—or would you have liked them to play—in this realization?

Friends provide a support base to deal with reality. We do not deal with reality either because we do not see it or we see it and are unable or unwilling to deal with it. Many times we know there is something wrong, but we cannot find it in ourselves to break away or do the right thing. In these situations, friends often provide a support base to get us though.

3. When have you relied on friends to help you through some of life's hard times, perhaps even the end of a dating relationship?

4. How did your friends support you through this time?

Friends help you stay connected to all parts of you. A good relationship helps us to become more of who God made us to be, not less. If you are losing yourself in a relationship, friends can help you stay connected to the things you were connected with before you started dating.

5. When, if ever, have you lost parts of yourself in a dating rela-
    tionship or perhaps even in a friendship? What parts did you
    lose?

Friends help us stay grounded in spiritual values that make life work. Our values are the architecture of life. They shape the way our life is going to be. When we begin to let our values slip, our life takes a direction that does not have a good end.

6. What values form the architecture of your life? List eight or ten.

7. In what ways might a dating relationship tempt you to com-
    promise on these values? Thinking about this in advance may
    help you avoid some heartache.

A FEW MORE THOUGHTS ON...
HOPE IN YOUR DATING LIFE

Hope is one of the greatest _____ (1 Co-
rinthians 13:13). The kind of hope God wants us to have is the
kind that "does not _____" (Romans 5:5), the
kind that is based on the love that God has for us. But the Bible
speaks of another kind of hope as well. It is the hope that "makes
the heart _____" (Proverbs 13:12), hope that is
never realized, hope that does not give life. What is the role of
hope in dating? When can we have hope that the person we are
with is going to change?

To determine whether your hope is merited, consider two
truths. First, it is _____ to continue to do the same
thing expecting different results. Second, the best predictor of the
_____, without some intervening variable, is the
_____. These two truths can help you determine
whether your current hope is merited. Be _____
with yourself.

Hope is a virtue. Hope should be based on _____.
Hope can be distorted and lead to a broken heart. As you date, hope
in _____, hope in his principles, hope in people of trustworthy _____, and hope in your own _____.
Those are truly good reasons for hope. But don't throw hope away
on things which have no reality behind them. That kind of hope
makes the heart sick.

LET'S TALK
Good Hope or Bad Hope?

DIRECTIONS

1. The leader will divide you into four groups and assign each group a scenario and accompanying questions.

2. Read through the scenario and discuss the questions, allowing everyone in the group to share. As before, italicized questions are part of your "Boundary Building" exercise, so disregard them for now.

3. The scenarios and each group's responses will be reviewed with the large group after the exercise is over.

4. You will have 5 minutes to complete this exercise.

SCENARIO 1

The person you love treats you in a way that you cannot live with.

Jayne was delightful. Her quick wit was part of her charm— at first. But at one point Scott realized that too often her sharpness seemed to bring laughs at his expense. He was frustrated that every time he tried to talk to her about it, she made a joke. He had even tried writing Jayne a letter to explain how her humor affected him and point to specific situations. Scott wasn't even sure she had taken the time to read the letter.

1. What could Jayne have done to give Scott hope that things were going to be different? What words and/or behaviors would have shown that she was taking ownership, that she wanted to be different, or that she had indeed heard what Scott was trying to tell her?

2. What advice would you give Scott?

3. *If the person you love treats you in a way that you cannot live with, how are you dealing with it? Is your hope merited? What reason has he or she given you to hope that things are going to be different? Is that reason sustainable?*

4. Are you seeing evidence of true change and growth? Is there more ownership, a growth path, hunger for change, involvement in some system of change, repentance, or other fruits of a change of direction? Is there self-motivation for change, or is it all coming from you?

SCENARIO 2

A person you are dating says he or she "likes you" or "loves you" but is not "in love with you" and wants more time to see where the relationship is going.

Luke knew right away that there was something different about Kelli. She had a way of bringing out the best in him. She clearly seemed to enjoy being with him, she laughed at his jokes, she listened carefully as he described the challenges of his teaching day, and she readily helped him grade papers (what a lame excuse to be together, but she offered!). He knew she readily canceled plans with her girlfriends when he called at the last minute. All of these signs—and more—were very encouraging. But still Kelli insisted that she loved Luke but wasn't "in love" with him.

1. What might be behind Kelli's word game? Imagine what she might be feeling or fearing.

2. Which of the following pieces of advice would you give Luke? Why?

   — Tell Kelli that you have enjoyed your time together, but you are developing more feelings than she is, so you do not see any reason in going forward if it is not mutual. Then end the dating relationship.

   — End the relationship and don't go back for any reason.

   — Tell Kelli that you are willing to continue if she feels like more time is going to help.

   — Continue with your eyes wide open.

3. *If Luke's situation is a lot like your current situation, have you tried to take the relationship to a different level from the "just friends" status? What did you do and how were your efforts received?*

4. If you have let your feelings be known, but nothing seems to have changed, you (like Luke) could do one of the following. Which will you choose and why?
   —*Tell your date that you have enjoyed your time together, but you are developing more feelings than he or she is, so you*

do not see any reason in going forward if it is not mutual. Then end the dating relationship.

— End the relationship and don't go back for any reason.

— Tell your date that you are willing to continue if he or she feels like more time is going to help.

— Continue with your eyes wide open.

SCENARIO 3

Your dating partner won't commit to the relationship's future.

Sherry knew Tim loved her. Why else would he spend most of his free time with her? Why else would he take her on such great getaways and regularly surprise her with such expensive gifts? And why else would he have been so helpful these last three months since her mom broke her hip and that whole nursing home nightmare had begun? So why, Sherry wondered, wouldn't Tim commit to the relationship's future? Their lives certainly seemed to be getting more and more entwined, but Tim made it clear he didn't want to talk about the "M" word!

1. Why might Tim be reluctant to commit to his future with Sherry?

2. What advice would you give Sherry? Why?

3. *If you are currently facing this situation, why might your partner be reluctant? Is he certain about you but doubtful about the timing? Or is he dealing with commitment phobia or commitment allergy? Support your answer with specifics— and get a friend's perspective too.*

4. Is the handwriting on the wall? Is it time to pull the plug? What will you do to let your support system do its job for you?

SCENARIO 4

You want a friend to like you in a different way, but it is not happening.

Katie had known Garrett for a long time and in a variety of settings, and the more she saw of him, the more she was attracted to him. He'd always been a great friend, helping her move into her new apartment, calling her when there was another opening on the church's coed softball team, and always willing to grab the latest Tom Hanks movie with her. And a few months ago when Garrett spent that Saturday with her and her three young and less-than-well-behaved nephews, she knew she was falling in love. He was great with kids! But, despite Katie's wish for their friendship to become something more, nothing had happened.

1. What advice would you give Katie? What could she do or say that might spark a change?

2. What risk does Katie take if she chooses to do something different in the relationship in hopes of bringing about a change? How could she decide if the possible gain is worth the risk?

3. *If you currently find yourself in this situation, what statement (openness and honesty about what you're thinking and feeling? discussing what dating each other would be like?) or action (greater knowledge of each other? spending more time together?) might be an "intervening variable" that sparks a change?*

4. Are you doing something different in the relationship that could bring about change? Or are you continuing to do the same things expecting different results? If you have not tried something different, there may be some hope if you change.

VIDEO SEGMENT
Boundaries on Blame

- We're part of a dating problem when we don't put boundaries on blame.

- Blaming is ascribing responsibility to someone for a fault. When we accuse another of a problem, we are blaming.

- Blame is not bad in and of itself; it has a good function. Blame separates out who is truly responsible for what in a problem, so that we are able to know how to solve it. Blame helps differentiate between what is our fault and what is another's.

- The blame that kills a good dating relationship is when one person sees herself as blameless and attributes almost all of the problems in the relationship to the other person.

- Blame can be one of the gravest problems we face spiritually and emotionally. It keeps us more concerned about being "good" than about being honest.

- Learn to humbly listen to correction and restrain the urge to react in blame. Let blame signal you to see if you are afraid, feel judged, or are sad about a fault. Be more concerned about your own soul's state than that of your date's. Also, ask those you trust to let you know when you play the blame game.

- Accept what is negative about your date and work with the realities instead of staying locked in protest, argument, and blame.

- Be a forgiver—make mutual forgiveness a part of your dating relationships.

A FEW MORE THOUGHTS ON ...
BLAME

The Blame Game

• Blaming has the power to negate the growth of _____ in a dating relationship.

• You don't even have to verbally blame the other person to ruin the relationship. Blaming can be done in your _____, without your speaking a word.

• Ultimately, blame is its own and only _____.

• Finally, blame can kill a dating relationship when the injured person takes on an attitude of _____ to her offender.

Five Guidelines for Curing Blame

1. Become _____. The most important solution is to actively observe your own soul for faults and weaknesses.

2. Relate to both the _____ and _____ of your date. It is hard to maintain a blaming stance if you keep the good parts of your date in mind as much as you do the bad parts.

3. Set _____ instead of _____. Many times people blame because it is the only way they can protest what the other person is doing.

4. _____. Another reason people continually blame is that they have difficulty forgiving their date. Forgiveness is canceling a debt that someone owes.

5. _____. While forgiveness is objective in nature, grief is its emotional component. When we cancel a debt, we are letting go of the right to demand revenge. That letting go brings loss and a feeling of sadness.

ON YOUR OWN
Curing Blame

DIRECTIONS

As part of your "Boundary Building" exercise this week, consider the "Five Guidelines for Curing Blame" and work through the following questions.

1. Which of your own faults and weaknesses—especially those that greatly impact your friendships and dating relationships—are you very much aware of?

2. What will you do to become aware of your faults if, up to this point, you have chosen to remain blind to them? Whom, for instance, will you trust to speak the truth in love to you?

3. Explore why it is difficult for you to look at your faults. Do you feel easily condemned or "bad"? Do you feel all alone when your faults are evident? Have you not had much experience in taking criticism and feeling loved? Begin to work on these issues.

4. Why is relating to both the good and bad of your date not denial—and why is chronic blaming closer to denial?

5. When, if ever, have you been very aware of a date or a friend accepting the bad as well as the good in you? How did you know about that person's awareness of your bad? How does being accepted despite your bad strengthen a relationship?

6. Think about a dating relationship or friendship where you were the "blamee." What boundaries could the blamer have been working on setting instead of merely blaming you?

7. When, if ever, have you found it easier to blame instead of set boundaries? Be specific about the dynamics of the friendship or dating relationship.

8. Blaming never really solves the problem you have. Limits often do, and thus eliminate the need for blaming in the first place. When, if ever, have you experienced or seen limits solve a problem in a dating relationship or friendship? Be specific about the work of setting boundaries and how those boundaries were received.

9. When, if ever, have you felt blamed rather than forgiven? What impact did that have on the relationship? And when, if ever, have you chosen to blame rather than to forgive? Why did you make that choice, and what were the results of your decision?

10. Our advice is to set limits on what can change, and to deal with and forgive what will not. In what current relationship, dating or otherwise, do you have an opportunity to forgive? Make it a topic of prayer and action.

11. While forgiveness is objective in nature, grief is its emotional component. When we cancel a debt, we are letting go of the right to demand revenge. That letting go brings loss and a feeling of sadness. When, if ever, have you lost the battle for a person to change, to see things your way, or to understand just how much she hurt you? What did you do with your anger at that

loss—hold on to it or let go of it and grieve? What impact did your choice have on the relationship?

12. Every day God lets go and feels sad about how we choose to conduct our lives (Matthew 23:37). What does this truth help you see about yourself and about how God would have you treat other people?

Boundary Building

This week spend some time answering the questions in "Safe Dating," "Good Hope or Bad Hope?" and "Curing Blame." You might also spend some time in prayer asking God to show you both where you are contributing to any current dating problems and what he would have you do about that.

Suggested Reading

For more thoughts on this session's topics, read chapters 12, 13, and 14 in *Boundaries in Dating*: "Don't Get Kidnapped," "Kiss False Hope Good-bye," and "Boundaries on Blame." For a more thorough self-evaluation, look at chapters 12, 13, and 14 in the *Boundaries in Dating Workbook*.

Session Nine

Solving Dating Problems When Your Date Is the Problem

OVERVIEW

In this session you will

- Learn how to say no to your date's disrespect.

- Recognize the importance of setting limits on what behaviors you'll tolerate and not tolerate.

- Use boundaries as tools for both diagnosing the character of your relationship and for laying down consequences so that the relationship can improve.

- Acknowledge that everyone needs to be involved in the process of spiritual growth.

VIDEO SEGMENT
Say No to Disrespect

• Respect is the ability to value another's experience. Empathy is the ability to feel another's experience, especially a painful one. Any relationship needs both. You may not be able to actually empathize with someone, but you can always take a position of respect for them.

• Disrespect is a serious obstacle to closeness, intimacy, and a couple's chances for marital success. When respect is present, the other person feels that he can be free to be who he is.

• A disrespectful relationship has to do, ultimately, with character. Disrespect can be caused by selfishness, control, lack of understanding, and other things.

• Respect and esteem your date's thoughts, feelings, and choices—and require that sort of treatment from him. Address early in the relationship any disrespect you notice.

• Don't fight fire with fire. Start with vulnerability and state your desire for the relationship to be better.

• See if you are making it easier to be disrespected by putting yourself in a position of inferiority in the relationship and letting yourself be treated as such.

• Make a distinction between differences and disrespect. You can disagree and even get angry with each other *respectfully*.

LET'S TALK

What Cures Disrespect

DIRECTIONS

1. The leader will be dividing you into seven groups and assigning each group one cure for disrespect listed below.

2. Each group will have about 5 minutes to plan and practice a one- to two-minute role-play based on their assigned "cure." After the group is called back together, each small group will present their scene to the rest of the class.

3. The "For personal reflection" question is part of this week's "Boundary Building" exercise, so please disregard it for now.

7 CURES FOR DISRESPECT

1. **Deal with it right away.** What conversation might happen on the second or third date? Be sure to speak the truth in love.

2. **Get to know your date in the context of other relationships.** What realization might you have after seeing your date interact with other people? Are you the guilty party whose demands are too high? Is your date treating you differently than he treats others? In role-playing, share with the disrespectful date your insights about the difference in his or her behavior in the context of other relationships.

3. **Say no to your date's preference.** This isn't as easy as it may sound. Show how the disrespecter will try to change your no to yes.

4. **Address the disrespect problem.** See if the disrespect is rooted in ignorance by telling the disrespecter that you feel controlled, dismissed, or unheard. Have the disrespecter respond with rationalization, denial, blame, or an apology and a real desire to change.

5. **Clarify.** Address what bothers you about the disrespectful behavior, how you feel when you are disrespected, how you would like to be treated, and what you will do if things do not change. Show both an effective way of saying these things and the disrespecter's response (rationalization, denial, blame, or an apology and a real desire to change.)

6. **Bring others in.** Get support, feedback, and reality testing from safe friends. Role-play a conversation between a person who is being disrespected and a safe friend who can offer support and reality testing.

7. **Own your own part.** Role-play a person being disrepected talking to a safe friend and recognizing the guilt of not saying anything, which can imply consent; of treating the disrespect lightly; of vacillating between doing nothing and being enraged; or of making it all his fault and problem instead of his date's. Have the safe friend offer some helpful input.

For Personal Reflection

Think about disrespect from the other perspective. What disrespectful behaviors, if any, might you be guilty of in a dating relationship (past or present) or a friendship? The following list of actions that show respect might help you see where you may fall short.

- You hear and value your date's opinion.
- You validate differences and disagreements.
- You esteem your date's choices, even the wrong ones.
- You consider your date's feelings.
- You confront the other person respectfully, you do not talk down to them or baby them.

A FEW MORE THOUGHTS ON...
GETTING WHAT YOU TOLERATE

Patience and the ability to overlook some offenses are wonderful qualities (Proverbs 19:11), but overlooking certain negative character patterns long-term can lead to a real problem. Some weeds are worth confronting. The following should not be tolerated for very long:

- Being inconsiderate regarding _____ or commitments

- Not following through on _____ or commitments

- _____ comments that are degrading or otherwise hurtful

- Pushing for _____ relationship past where you allow

- Unfair or irresponsible _____ dealings

- _____ attitudes

- Other consistent ways of _____ your feelings that are clearly his or her fault and not your own sensitivities

- _____ behavior

VIDEO SEGMENT
Set Up a Detention Hall

- Though no one has the power to fix anyone else, you do have the power to respond in healthy ways to your date when problems arise.

- Some conflict is normal. Problems, including boundary conflicts, are a normal part of relationships.

- Don't wait to set a limit until there is a huge problem or crisis in your love life. Boundaries should be woven into the fabric of your daily life and relationships.

- See boundaries as tools for diagnosing the character of your date and of the relationship. Basically, think about boundaries as preserving the relationship, not ending it.

- Approach your date from a stance of love, respect, and mutuality. Be very specific with your date about the boundary problem.

- Have these seven things in place as you go through the boundary-setting process.

  1. *Stay connected* to good people who will stand by you when conflicts arise.

  2. *Avoid reactive friends* who idealize you as an innocent victim or who are critical and judgmental of you. Find mature people who are "for" both of you and can see both sides of the issue.

  3. *Expect negative reactions.* Don't be surprised by anger or defensiveness, but demand respect.

  4. *Empathize with the struggle,* acknowledging that what you are requiring is difficult.

  5. *Be patient* and allow time for God's process to take hold. But recognize also that patience has an end; it does not wait forever without a good reason.

  6. *Question his motives.* It is important that your date be changing because of his relationship with God, because it

is the right thing to do, and because he doesn't want to hurt you—and not changing simply because he wants you back.

7. *Provide a way back to normal relationships* by letting your date know that the consequences are not necessarily permanent. But stay out of the parental role—be his equal!

• If you have boundary struggles with someone you are involved with, it makes sense to set up consequences aimed at dealing with the problem.

• Everyone needs to be involved in the process of spiritual growth. This means being in a process in which the person brings his struggles, weaknesses, and vulnerabilities to God and some safe people on an ongoing basis.

A FEW MORE THOUGHTS ON . . . SETTING APPROPRIATE CONSEQUENCES

Here are four guidelines for setting appropriate consequences:

1. Be motivated by _____ and truth, not _____.
    Think of consequences as protecting you and giving your date a
    chance to change.

2. _____ the ultimate consequence: breaking off the
    relationship prematurely. Breaking up is not truly a conse-
    quence because it ends rather than cures a relationship.

3. Think _____. Put yourself in your date's
    shoes. How would you feel with various consequences?

4. Use _____ as your guide. Make the consequences
    fit, as much as possible, with natural consequences. Get your-
    self out of the way as much as possible so your date doesn't see
    you as the problem, but sees his relationship with reality as
    the problem.

LET'S TALK

Boundaries Are Not Consequences

DIRECTIONS

1. The leader will divide you into four groups and assign each group a scenario from below.
2. Considering the scenario to which you've been assigned, answer the two questions at the bottom of the page.
3. You will have 5 minutes to complete this exercise.

DATING SCENARIOS

1. Your date is always late.
2. Your date wants to stay in touch with former boyfriends/ girl-friends.
3. Your boyfriend/girlfriend wants to borrow money from you.
4. Your boyfriend/girlfriend has a secret drug or alcohol problem.

   What might be some appropriate consequences that would improve this situation? List two or three.

   Review the four guidelines for setting appropriate consequences. How did the consequences you just established for your hypo-thetical situation measure up? What tweaking is needed to make those consequences more appropriate?

Boundary Building

Look again at the list on page 116 of some things in a relationship that should not be tolerated for very long.

1. When have you been guilty of these behaviors, if any? What does that fact reveal about the growing up you need to do—and what steps will you take toward a more godly and mature character?
2. When, in the past, have you tolerated any of these behaviors? What would you now do differently in that situation?
3. What appropriate and effective consequences might you establish in each situation you just referred to?

Also, take time to answer the "For personal reflection" question in the "What Cures Disrespect" exercise.

Suggested Reading

For more thoughts on this session's topics, read chapters 15, 16, and 18 in *Boundaries in Dating:* "Say No to Disrespect," "Nip It in the Bud," and "Set Up a Detention Hall." For a more thorough self-evaluation, look at chapters 15, 16, and 18 in the *Boundaries in Dating Workbook*.

Session Ten

Appropriate Physical Limits— and a Few Closing Words

OVERVIEW

In this session you will

- Look closely at 1 Thessalonians 4:3–8, God's "big rule" of reserving sex for marriage.

- Consider five reasons why God calls for sexual abstinence outside of marriage.

- Hear gracious words about the forgiveness available to you if you have already said yes to sex outside of marriage.

- Evaluate six critical measures of a good dating relationship to help you make sure that the good things God has designed for life are actually occurring in dating.

VIDEO SEGMENT
The Big Rule—and Why

- God wants people to reserve sex for marriage. This rule is found, among other places, in 1 Thessalonians 4:3–8:

  It is God's will that you should be sanctified: that you should avoid sexual immorality; that each of you should learn to control his own body in a way that is holy and honorable, not in passionate lust like the heathen, who do not know God; and that in this matter no one should wrong his brother or take advantage of him. The Lord will punish men for all such sins, as we have already told you and warned you. For God did not call us to be impure, but to live a holy life. Therefore he who rejects this instruction does not reject man but God, who gives you his Holy Spirit.

- This statement of God's rule contains five reasons why he calls for sexual abstinence outside marriage. First, Paul calls God's people to "control [their] body in a way that is holy and honorable" (1 Thessalonians 4:4). *Holiness* means "purity" and "being set aside for a high purpose," and *honor* means things like "dignity, precious, of high price or value, or high esteem." God is saying that sex is not a casual thing. To spend sex casually or unwisely is foolish, and you will be cheated in the end.

- Paul also says, "Each of you should learn to control his own body" (1 Thessalonians 4:4). Control of one's own body is a sign that a person is capable of delay of gratification and self-control, which are prerequisites of the ability to love.

- Paul teaches against passionate lust (1 Thessalonians 4:5), a lust for that which is forbidden outside of marriage. Passionate lust splits you from your real heart, your mind, your values, and the life you truly desire. Lust gets momentary fulfillment at the expense of lasting gain.

- Paul also teaches that when sex occurs outside of marriage, someone is always wronged (1 Thessalonians 4:6). When someone sleeps with a person to whom he or she is not married, he or she is hurting that person. If you say you are a person of love, then you won't wrong someone you love. You will wait. And vice versa, do not allow anyone else to wrong you. Love waits to give, but lust can't wait to get.

- Paul teaches us that the authority for sexuality belongs not to us, but to God. God wants to be accepted as he really is, rules and all. When someone rewrites God's values, they are not accepting who he really is.

- It is difficult to keep someone out of your heart who has invaded your body. That in itself is another reason to say no to sex outside of marriage.

- Sexuality is a part of God's good creation. But as you embrace your sexuality, do so with self-control, sanctity, high esteem, lovingly and not lustfully, sacrificially and not "wronging" someone, and in submission to God.

ON YOUR OWN

Five Reasons for the Big Rule

DIRECTIONS

On your own, work through the questions below. What you don't get to will be your "Boundary Building" exercise this week. You will have 15 minutes to complete this exercise.

Holy and honorable. Sex is set apart for a purpose and has great value. It is for a lifelong commitment and needs to be esteemed. In a physical and spiritual sense, it is all you can give someone. Therefore, it should not be given away lightly.

1. What differences exist between a break up when the couple was sleeping together and a break up when the couple wasn't? Answer this question based on either what you've seen or what you've experienced.

2. Because sex and the heart are connected, people often feel as if they lose a part of themselves when a lover ends a relationship. Why do so many of us learn that the hard way—from our own experience rather than from people who have gone before us?

Self-control. Choose someone who can delay gratification for the sake of you and the relationship. Boundaries with sex are a surefire test to know if someone loves you for you.

3. A committed relationship calls for sacrifice. In friendships as well as dating relationships, what kinds of sacrifices have you seen made—or perhaps made yourself—in any of the following areas?

Time

Money

Getting one's own way

Working out conflict

4. What kind of sacrifices are involved in respecting boundaries about sex?

5. What is a good response to "If you love me, you will [have sex]"?

Passionate lust. Instead of expressing love through sex, the luster replaces love with sex. Lust gets momentary fulfillment at the expense of lasting gain. Furthermore—as countless married people have found out—the person they married who could not wait was incapable of real relationship.

6. Lusters have divided souls and do not develop deeper aspects of themselves which are necessary for a lasting relationship. What undeveloped skills can sex outside of marriage keep a person from dealing with? What activities can sex replace?

7. Your sexual abstinence is a great way to find out how fulfilled you are as a person. When, if ever, have you used sex to replace relationship? What does that action tell you about your deep longings and unhealed hurts?

Wronging someone. If you say you are a person of love, then you won't wrong someone you love. You will wait. And vice versa, do not allow anyone else to wrong you. Love waits to give.

8. If you have slept with someone outside of marriage, which of the following hurts have you experienced as a result?

   • Your soul and body split: your body gave 100 percent, and your soul was connected to some lesser degree.

   • You cheapened a very precious part of yourself and someone else.

   • You caused a person to not develop deeper aspects of relatedness and spirituality.

   • You came between a person and God.

   • You helped a person deny hurt and pain.

   • You used someone for your own pleasure and lust, and that is a long way from love.

   • While you used them, you kept them from finding someone who will truly value them.

   • You set them up for heartbreak and devastation if you break up and take with you something so precious.

9. If you have pressured someone to sleep with you outside of marriage, what hurts listed in question 8 might you have inflicted? What, if anything, have you done to seek forgiveness—God's as well as that person's?

Accepting God. God wants to be accepted as he really is, rules and all. When someone rewrites his values, they are not accepting who he really is. So be sure you're trusting a person who truly trusts God. If he or she is, that person will uphold God's value of sex within marriage.

10. Why is it important—for a dating relationship now and for a possible marriage in the future—to see whether a person submits to the Lord? Put differently, what kinds of problems will arise if your date submits only when God's way doesn't interfere with his or her desires?

11. What does the litmus test of your sexuality tell you about yourself, your spirituality, and your submission to the God of the Bible rather than to a God you're re-creating to fit your needs and desires? Are you walking humbly with your God (Micah 6:8)? What repentance is in order?

A FEW MORE THOUGHTS ON ...
THE BOUNDARY OF FORGIVENESS

If you ask God to _____ you through Jesus, he sees you as a completely new person. You are clean, washed with pure water. Whatever you might have done is forgotten and put away as the east is from the west. As Paul says, "there is...no _____" for those who have asked for the forgiveness that Jesus gives (Romans 8:1).

Your past failure does not have to doom you to further sexual brokenness. Just because you have fallen in the past does not mean that you have ruined yourself and cannot _____ _____. You can become clean again. And as you do, you can _____ to remaining pure and enjoying all the benefits of that state:

- You can develop the _____ life and your ability to _____.

- You can know if someone really loves you.

- You can learn how to _____ gratification and _____ to others.

- You can have your underlying splits, needs, and hurts _____ and fulfilled so that you will not have unsatisfying relationships.

- You can finally give up being God and allow him to be _____ for you.

If you know you are forgiven, that clean slate is a powerful _____. Dating can now be about building deeper things than a one-night experience. It can be a place of _____ instead of brokenness.

VIDEO SEGMENT

Critical Measures of a Good Dating Relationship

- Learning to have good boundaries in dating is work and takes some time, but it pays off as you understand how to better conduct your dating life to develop love, freedom, and responsibility in both you and whomever you are dating.

- Boundaries in dating is about becoming a truthful, caring, responsible, and free person who encourages growth in those with whom you are in contact. The following six critical measures are meant to make sure that the good things God has designed in dating are actually occurring:

  1. Is dating growing me up?
  2. Is dating bringing me closer to God?
  3. Am I more able to have good relationships?
  4. Am I picking better dates over time?
  5. Am I a better potential mate?
  6. Am I enjoying the ride?

LET'S TALK

How Are You Doing?

DIRECTIONS

Pair up with someone sitting near you and discuss the six questions found on page 131 and the questions below. You will have 10 minutes to complete this exercise.

1. If you've been dating, what aspects of your dating are you pleased with? What points do you want to work on?

2. Whether you have an active dating life or are about to start dating or start dating again, what specific goals do you have for your dating life?

3. Whatever your situation, what about this book's perspective on dating has convicted you? Challenged you? Encouraged you?

Boundary Building

Continue the boundary building work you've begun by completing the "On Your Own: Five Reasons for the Big Rule" questions. Remember that assignments like these are actually projects for life, pointing you to health and growth and living the way God has designed you to live.

Suggested Reading

For more thoughts on this session's topics, read "Set Appropriate Physical Limits" (chapter 17) and the conclusion of *Boundaries in Dating*. For a more thorough self-evaluation, look at chapter 17 and the conclusion in the *Boundaries in Dating Workbook*.

For information on books, resources, or speaking engagements:

Cloud-Townsend Resources
3176 Pullman Avenue, Suite 104
Costa Mesa, CA 92626
Phone: 1-800-676-HOPE (4673)
Web: www.cloudtownsend.com

About the Writer

Lisa Guest writes, edits, and develops curriculum from her home in Irvine, California, where she lives with her husband and two children. She has written two books, *Small Miracles* and *A Mother's Love*. She enjoys swimming, reading, and playing with her kids.

How a Well-Timed "No" Can Triple the Joy of Saying "Yes"

Boundaries

(Revised)

When to Say Yes, When to Say No to Take Control of Your Life

Dr. Henry Cloud &
Dr. John Townsend
0-310-22362-8

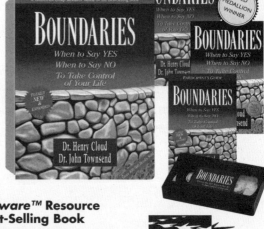

**A Zondervan*Groupware*™ Resource
Based on the Best-Selling Book**

—Totally new and expanded
—Over 400,000 books sold

Zondervan*Groupware*

Interactive Format—Specially Designed for Groups of Any Size

Do you have trouble saying no? • **Can you set limits and still be a loving person?**
Are you in control of your life? • What are legitimate boundaries?
Do people take advantage of you?
How do you answer someone who wants your time, love, energy, and money?

Dr. Henry Cloud and Dr. John Townsend offer biblically based answers to these tough questions as they show us how to set healthy boundaries with our parents, our spouses, our children, our friends, our coworkers, and even ourselves. This compelling, nine-part video resource helps us define and maintain the clear personal boundaries that are essential to a healthy and balanced Christian life.

Applying the proven "group-interactive" format designed to enhance participation and learning among small-group members, *Boundaries* helps us discover the impact of boundaries on all areas of our lives.
It shows us:

- How to know where our responsibilities begin and end
- How to be free to choose the right things for ourselves in the light of God's will
- How to say no to irresponsible or controlling people
- How to say yes for the right reasons
- How to deal with guilt and the fear of losing love

With brief video dramatizations and discussion jump-starters by Drs. Cloud and Townsend, the *Boundaries* Zondervan*Groupware* resource provides everything needed to successfully conduct nine lively, life-changing small-group sessions.

The Boundaries Groupware kit includes:
1 94-minute video
This nine-part video features the wisdom and insight of Dr. Cloud and Dr. Townsend, popular speakers and experts in the integration of Scripture and psychology. Interspersed are helpful real-life vignettes of people struggling to establish and live by godly boundaries.

1 Leader's (Revised) Guide*
This comprehensive, user-friendly guide provides all the information you need to lead your group through the nine sessions of this course.

1 Participant's (Revised) Guide*
This guide provides valuable notes and practical exercises (small-group discussion starters, independent Bible studies, "Boundary Building" questions, etc.) that will help individuals apply to their lives the principles they learn.

1 *Boundaries* hardcover book*
In this longtime best-seller, Dr. Henry Cloud and Dr. John Townsend offer biblically based guidelines for setting healthy boundaries with our parents, spouses, children, friends, coworkers, and even ourselves.

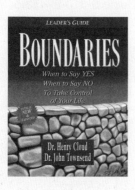

Boundaries interactive sessions include:
- What Is a Boundary?
- Understanding Boundaries
- The Laws of Boundaries, Part I
- The Laws of Boundaries, Part II
- Myths About Boundaries
- Boundary Conflicts, Part I
- Boundary Conflicts, Part II
- Boundary Successes, Part I
- Boundary Successes, Part II

*Additional copies may be purchased separately

"Dr. Henry Cloud and Dr. John Townsend have great insight and practical wisdom into the God-given gift of *Boundaries*. As they discuss how to take personal responsibility for and ownership of our lives, they give us hope that we can not just survive but thrive!"

Josh McDowell *Author and speaker*

Best-Selling Boundaries resources available from Dr. Henry Cloud and Dr. John Townsend

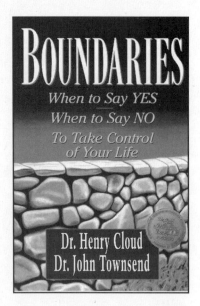

BOUNDARIES

Presents a biblical treatment of boundaries, identifies how boundaries are developed and how they become injured, shows Christian misconceptions of their function and purpose, and gives a program for developing and maintaining healthy limits.

Hardcover 0-310-58590-2
Audio Pages 0-310-58598-8
Workbook 0-310-49481-8
Zondervan*Groupware*™ 0-310-22362-8
Leader's Guide 0-310-22452-7
Participant's Guide 0-310-22453-5

BOUNDARIES IN MARRIAGE

Helps you understand the friction points or serious hurts and betrayals in your marriage—and move beyond them to the mutual care, respect, affirmation, and intimacy you both long for.

Hardcover 0-310-22151-X
Audio Pages 0-310-22549-3
Workbook 0-310-22875-1

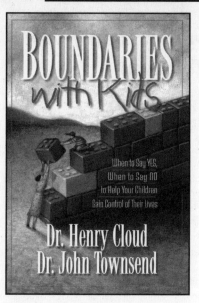

BOUNDARIES WITH KIDS

Helps parents set boundaries with their children and helps them teach their children the concept of boundaries.

Hardcover 0-310-20035-0
Audio Pages 0-310-59560-6
Workbook 0-310-22349-0

BOUNDARIES IN DATING

Road map to the kind of enjoyable, rewarding dating that can take you from weekends alone to a lifetime with the soul mate you've longed for.

Softcover 0-310-20034-2
Audio pages 0-310-24055-0
Workbook 0-310-23330-5
Zondervan*Groupware™* 0-310-23873-0
Leader's Guide 0-310-23874-9
Participant's Guide 0-310-23875-7

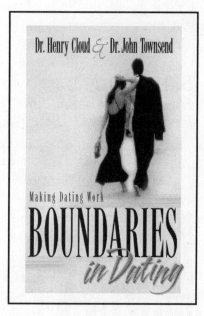

Pick up a copy today at your favorite bookstore!

ZondervanPublishingHouse
Grand Rapids, Michigan 49530
http://www.zondervan.com

Other Great Resources by Dr. Henry Cloud and Dr. John Townsend

RAISING GREAT KIDS
A Comprehensive Guide to Parenting with Grace and Truth

Hardcover 0-310-22569-8
Softcover 0-310-23549-9
Audio Pages 0-310-22572-8
Workbook for Parents of Preschoolers 0-310-22571-X
Workbook for Parents of School-Age Children 0-310-23452-2
Workbook for Parents of Teenagers 0-310-23437-9
Zondervan*Groupware*™ for Parents of Preschoolers
0-310-23238-4
Parents of Preschoolers Leader's Guide 0-310-23296-1
Parents of Preschoolers Participant's Guide 0-310-23295-3

SAFE PEOPLE
How to Find Relationships That Are Good for You and Avoid Those That Aren't

Softcover 0-310-21084-4
Mass Market 0-310-49501-6
Audio Pages 0-310-59568-1

CHANGES THAT HEAL
How to Understand Your Past to Ensure a Healthier Future
Dr. Henry Cloud

Softcover 0-310-60631-4
Mass Market 0-310-21463-7
Audio Pages 0-310-20567-0
Workbook 0-310-60633-0

HIDING FROM LOVE

How to Change the Withdrawal Patterns
That Isolate and Imprison You
Dr. John Townsend

Softcover 0-310-20107-1
Workbook 0-310-23828-5

We all long to be cared for, but we prevent it by...

HIDING FROM LOVE

How to Change the
Withdrawal Patterns That Isolate
and Imprison You

Dr. John Townsend

Foreword by Paul Meier, M.D.

NOW WITH DISCUSSION GUIDE

The **MOM FACTOR**

Discover How To:
- Transform the Effects of the Past
  Say "No" to Your Mom Without Feeling Guilty
- Build a Healthy Relationship with Your Mom
  Improve All Your Relationships!

Dr. Henry Cloud
Dr. John Townsend

Authors of *Boundaries*

THE MOM FACTOR

Identifies six types of moms and shows how
they profoundly affect our lives.

Softcover 0-310-22559-0

TWELVE "CHRISTIAN" BELIEFS THAT CAN DRIVE YOU CRAZY

Relief from False Assumptions

Softcover 0-310-49491-5

NOW WITH DISCUSSION GUIDE

12 "Christian" Beliefs
That Can Drive You
Crazy
RELIEF FROM *False Assumptions*

Dr. Henry Cloud &
Dr. John Townsend

AUTHORS OF *BOUNDARIES*

Pick up a copy today at your favorite bookstore!

ZondervanPublishingHouse
Grand Rapids, Michigan 49530
http://www.zondervan.com

We want to hear from you. Please send your comments about this
book to us in care of the address below. Thank you.

ZondervanPublishingHouse
Grand Rapids, Michigan 49530
http://www.zondervan.com